The C   n university

V: ?

SIMON PATTERSON

BLACK-LIST

DAVID CAMPANY THE END

MADE WITH PANAVISION® CA

How does a film come to an end? It may be more complicated than we imagine. Think of a typical experience in your local cinema. The average film actually has a sort of compound ending, made up of several parts that are carefully choreographed. First, the plot will be resolved, more or less. The arrival of the words "The End" will then confirm this for you. Rarely do the words themselves introduce the conclusion – that would be too sudden. In effect, they are already the second ending. They will appear in the centre of the screen or rise from the bottom. What we see may be accompanied by a change in the soundtrack to what Hollywood calls exit music. This seems to belong to the film, but also apparently comes from outside of it, like a commentary. The end credits will follow. A black screen will be left behind as the final words leave the frame. Then the curtains will close. We are never permitted to see the final frame of celluloid pass through the projector's gate – that would be too "material", too anti-illusionistic and too hard on the eyes. As the curtains close, lights will illuminate the auditorium, usually gradually, but not as slowly as they were dimmed at the beginning. By this time most of the audience will have left their seats, if not the cinema. Perhaps a few will remain for a short while. Finally, if you are still there, an usher will ask you to leave. Which of these events is the real ending? All of them and none of them.

A film's end credits are an example of what Gérard Genette has called paratexts – those supplementary bits and pieces that surround a work. They are not, strictly speaking, parts of the work, but they frame it for us (like the art catalogue essay). They give it a place, an order, a set of conventions and boundaries. And to some extent they may suggest or even dictate how we approach the work itself. Genette's specific interest was neither film nor art, but literature. He looked at all the possible paratexts we might find around a typical novel. In near endless detail he considered book jacket design, titles, authors' photographs and biographies, publishers' logos and notes, quotes from reviews, colophons, the ISBN and barcode, prefaces, the contents page, dedications, chapter titles and even the words The End (which few novels have). These are just some of the paratexts within the book itself. Genette added others that influence from a distance – publicity, reviews, gossip, recommendations, the author's reputation and all the rest. So much for a work "speaking for itself". We can imagine the dozens of paratexts that surround a film.

End credits mark the transition between the film's celluloid paratext, the paratexts of the auditorium and the paratexts beyond in the culture at large. Their purpose is twofold. First there is the pragmatic and even ethical need to acknowledge those who made the work. Then there is the psychological function. The audience suspends its disbelief in order to immerse itself in the filmic illusion. End credits help to bring the film back to a prosaic level, while smoothing the audience's passage from one mental state to another – from the world of the movie to the world itself. You cannot see a film as an illusion and as a material object at the same time. It requires either a sudden jolt or a gradual transition from one to

the other. This is why certain strands of avant-garde cinema became obsessed with trying to demystify the illusion with self-reflexive shock tactics and alienating tricks. It is also the reason why even the most basic closure of a movie is made up of all those incremental transitions. Like sleepwalkers, we must be awoken gently or not at all.

Of course it is not always like this. Sometimes we want to be "in" the film long after it has finished. Its closure and our closure are not quite the same thing. We may sit there in denial or reflection, giving our mind and body time to make their own transition. We may read the end credits out of interest, guilt, respect, or merely as something to keep doing with our eyes. We may take the darkness that accompanies them as a subdued period of grace (they are invariably white-on-black, not black-on-white).

In his little essay *On Leaving the Cinema*, Roland Barthes described his own body as it moved from the auditorium to the street. It was "a little numb, a little awkward, chilly…sleepy, soft, peaceful: limp as a sleeping cat". We can pull our body from its seat, but we might remain in a dream state. Sometimes we never quite sink into that semi-somnolence to begin with. At the end of a disappointing film we take without hesitation our first cue to leave.

Conventions are there to be broken. At the close of *The Birds* Alfred Hitchcock withheld the words The End. Moreover, the narrative refuses to resolve. The car containing the lead characters creeps through the menacing mass of birds until the sudden appearance of the Universal Studios logo across the screen. No credits, no words at all, just a fade to black. It is disquietingly abrupt. It is not even a cliffhanger. *The Birds* does not end; it stops. The reassurance of the words The End lies not just in their signalling that the film is over. They provide an official voice letting us know "this is how it is". Hitchcock's non-ending is more radical than the notorious "bad" conclusions of Hollywood movies from the 1970s, in which the good guys die and the bad guys win. It is more radical than non- or anti-narrative films. Just as there is no warning that harmless birds will turn on the characters, there is no indication that the filmic conventions will turn on us. Or perhaps there was. The ending echoes the paratextual subversion of the pre-release poster, which read: "*The Birds* is coming."

At the other end of the scale there is the long end credit sequence. The record is currently held by the second in *The Lord of the Rings* trilogy: nine minutes and 33 seconds. No doubt there were fans who watched right to the end. (What is a fan if not someone with a greater appetite for the paratexts than the rest of us?) No doubt many people worked on the film. But at nine and a half minutes it suggests the director was less interested in credits than in being sure his movie went on much longer than the audience. It says: "*The Lord of the Rings* is epic – it has more than you can take."

What about film and video in art? End credits are quite unusual in the gallery. They are not a conventional paratext of the artist's film. Certainly, some make their films alone, justifying art's stubborn insistence on the singular author-creator. Others opt for looped films without end or beginning, avoiding the problem of credits all together.

Or the credits may appear in other places: on an adjacent wall, in a gallery leaflet, or in a catalogue. Even so, cinema casts a long shadow over art. It poses a threat and a possibility. Sooner or later every artist must make their peace with cinema.

Similarly, the monochrome casts a long shadow over painting. Sooner or later every painter must make his or her peace with it. They work in the knowledge that it is a permanent fixture on the horizon of painting's options. Once the blank canvas and the black were accepted as art, every painting thereafter would be a painting on a painting. For the faint-hearted the monochrome represents the end. The bold have seen in it new beginnings writ large. Simon Patterson is bold and writes large on his monochromes. And the writing we see here speaks of cinema.

The flat blackness of the *Black-List* canvases speaks of art, of Modernism in transition between the painterly surface and the industrial surface. The writing – so clearly cinematic – introduces what used to be called a "double articulation": the already ambiguous black rectangles oscillate between canvas and screen. Their size is equally in-between. As screens they are small, as canvases they are large, alluding to that strange hybrid "home cinema". Moreover, look closely and we see the letters appear to glow, mimicking the poor transfer of big-screen celluloid to TV screen.

Hollywood is deeply anxious about endings. If a film gets bad notices in preview screenings, it can trigger an eleventh-hour crisis. Editors may be called upon to reshape the final minutes. Cast and crew can be obliged to reshoot. The irony is that our memory of movies rarely hinges on their endings. Indeed, the memory of film follows the dream logic of displacement and condensation. Isolated fragments are recalled, scenes are mentally stitched together out of order, moments and actors from different movies may find themselves combined in our minds. Patterson displaces and condenses different names and films. One painting looks like a credit list from Martin Scorsese's mob story *Goodfellas*. Almost. Scanning the others we may pick up names from the Cold War anti-communist tribunals. Those witch hunts led to a Hollywood blacklist of banned writers, directors and actors.

The old Cold War has been replaced by new wars and new paranoid fantasies. They are fuelled in part by the expanded realm of visual representations that now seems to govern political thought. This may be why we are seeing a tentative return to political film-making at the edges of Hollywood. It may also be why "the political" has returned equally tentatively to contemporary art. Our political present is haunted in so many ways by history. Our cultural present is similarly haunted, not least by the history of film and of art. It makes it all the more pertinent to look at the deep connection between looking back and the return of the repressed. After all, the repressed always returns out of place, just when we think things are over.

Titles by **ELAINE & SAUL BASS**

Unit Production Manager JOSEPH R. McCARTHY

First Assistant Director JOHN S. WOOD

Second Assistant Director PAT McCARRAN

CAST

James Conway	ROBERT DE NIRO
Henry Hill	RAY LIOTTA
Tommy DeVito	JOE PESCI
Karen Hill	KAREN MORLEY
Paul Cicero	EDWARD G. ROBINSON

Young Henry's Sister #1	DANIELA BARBOSA	Judge–1947	PAUL McISAAC
Young Henry's Sister #2	GINA MATTIA	Truck Driver at Diner	BOB GOLUB
Young Henry's Older Brother	JOEL CALENDRILLO	Fat Andy	MARC LAWRENCE
Young Michael	ANTHONY VALENTIN	Frankie the Wop	TONY LIP
Liquor Cop #1	EDWARD D. MURPHY	Freddy No Nose	MIKEY BLACK
Liquor Cop #2	ALBERT MALTZ	Pete The Killer	PETER CICALE
Mailman	ARTHUR MILLER	Jimmy Two Times	LARRY PARKS
Barbeque Wiseguy	ERASMUS C. ALFANIO	Man w/Coatrack	VINNY PASTORE
Bleeding Man	JOHN RANDOLPH	Henry's 40's crew	ANTHONY ALESSANDRO
Gambling Doorman	MANNY ALFARO		VICTOR COLICCHIO

Henry's Older Child (Jody)	STELLA KEITEL	Stacks' Girlfriend	BERLINDA TOLBERT
Henry's Baby (Ruth)	DOMINIQUE De VITO	Joe Buddha's Wife	NANCY ELEN CASSARO
Bar Patron	MICHAELANGELO GRAZIANO	Kid	ADAM WANDT
		Garbage Man	STERLING HAYDEN
Janice's Girlfriend #1	PAULA GALLO	Doctor	ISIAH WHITLOCK JR.
Janice's Girlfriend #2	NADINE KAY	Judy Hill @ 13 Years	ANNE REVERE
Bridal Shop Owner	SAM WANAMAKER	Ruth Hill @ 11 Years	ROSE HOBART
Florida Bookie	GENE KELLY	Arresting Narc	RONALD REAGAN
Bookie's Sister	JAMIE De ROY	Stuntpersons	
Judge–1951	JOE McCARTHY	HERBERT J. BIBERMAN	ALVAH BESSIE
Security Guard w/Lobsters	H. CLAY DEAR	SAMUEL ORNITZ	ADRIAN SCOTT
Drug Buyer	HUMPHREY BOGART	JOHN HOWARD LAWSON	LESTER COLE

Art Director	MAHER AHMAD
Set Decorator	ORSON BEAN
Art Department Researcher	ELIA KAZAN
Editor	JAMES KWEI
First Assistant Editor	JOHN HUSTON
Second Assistant Editor	PHIL BROWN
Assistant Editor	KENT BLOCHER
Script Supervisor	HERSCHEL BERNARDI
Music Editor	MARC BLITZSTEIN
Supervising Sound Editor	SKIP LIEVSAY
Supervising Dialogue Editor	LILLIAN HELLMAN
Dialogue Editors	MARISSA LITTLEFIELD

Foley Editors | BRUCE PROSS
| FRANK KERN
Assistant Sound Editors | ANNE SAWYER
| JOHN CROMWELL
| HOWARD DA SILVA
| WILLIAM WYLER
Production Sound Mixer | JAMES SABAT
Sound Recordist | FRANK GRAZIADEI
Boom Operator | LOUIS SABAT
Recording Mixer | PAUL JARRICO
Camera Operator | EDWARD DMYTRYK
First Assistant Camera | FLORIAN BALLHAUS
Second Assistant Camera | BOB MANCUSO

Second Assistant Camera BOB MANCUSO

Rigging Gaffer DALTON TRUMBO

Key Grip W. C. 'CHUNKY' HUSE
Best Boy Grip LEO PENN
Dolly Grip GERRIT GARRETSEN
Rigging Grip LAUREN BACALL

Special Effects Coordinator TERRY D. FRAZEE
Special Effects Foreman DONALD FRAZEE
Special Effects
GENO CRUM LOGAN FRAZEE

LLOYD GOUGH   JOSEPH LOSEY

Re-Recorded at TODD-AO

Transportation Coordinator BRYCE GUY WILLIAMS

Transportation Captains HOWARD BACHRACH

STEVE DUNCAN

Construction Coordinator ANTHONY LATTANZIO

Construction Foreman MIKE SFORZA

RING LARDNER JR.

Paint Foreman LARRY CLARK

Stage Painter JOE A. HAWTHORN

Stand-by Painters JOHN HINKLE

Black-List: Elaine & Saul Bass
2006
Acrylic on linen
195.6 × 304.8 cm

Black-List: Cast
2006
Acrylic on linen
195.6 × 304.8 cm

Black-List: Unit Production Manager
2006
Acrylic on linen
195.6 × 304.8 cm

Black-List: In Order of Appearance
2006
Acrylic on linen
195.6 × 304.8 cm

Black-List: Henry's Older Child
2006
Acrylic on linen
195.6 × 304.8 cm

Black-List: Assistant Sound Editors
2006
Acrylic on linen
195.6 × 304.8 cm

Black-List: Art Director
2006
Acrylic on linen
195.6 × 304.8 cm

Black-List: Rigging Gaffer
2006
Acrylic on linen
195.6 × 304.8 cm

Black-List: Re-recorded at
2006
Acrylic on linen
195.6 × 304.8 cm

Black-List: Motion Pictures Association
2006
Acrylic on linen
195.6 × 304.8 cm

SIMON PATTERSON

1967	Born in England
1985–86	Hertfordshire College of Art and Design, St. Albans
1986–89	Goldsmiths College, London, BA (Hons) Fine Art
1996	Short-listed for the Turner Prize

Lives and works in London.

SOLO EXHIBITIONS

2006	*Black-List,* Haunch of Venison, Zurich
2005	*High Noon,* Ikon Gallery Birmingham
	High Noon, Fruitmarket Gallery, Edinburgh
2004	*PaintstenroomS,* gSM, London
	Domini Canes – Hounds of God, Lowood Gallery and Kennels, Armathwaite, Cumbria
	Simon Patterson – New Work, Röntgenwerke, Tokyo
	Simon Patterson – 24 hours, Röntgenwerke, Tokyo
	Simon Patterson – Escape Routine, Röntgenwerke, Tokyo
2003	*Simon Patterson – Midway,* Röntgenwerke, Tokyo
2002	*Manned Flight, 1999—,* Studio 12, Artspace, Sydney
2001	*Simon Patterson,* Sies+Hoeke Galerie, Düsseldorf
	Le Match des couleurs, artconnexion, Lille
	Manned Flight, Lille
2000	*Simon Patterson,* VTO Gallery, London
	Manned Flight, 1999—, fig-1, London
1999	*Simon Patterson,* Magazin 4, Bregenz
1998	*Simon Patterson,* Mitaka City Art Center, Tokyo
	New Work, Röntgen Kunstraum, Tokyo
	Simon Patterson, Yamaguchi Gallery, Osaka
	Name Paintings, Kohji Ogura Gallery, Nagoya
1997	*Simon Patterson – Spies,* Gandy Gallery, Prague
	Wall Drawings, Kunsthaus, Zurich
	Simon Patterson, Röntgen Kunstraum, Tokyo
1996	*Simon Patterson,* MCA, Chicago
	Simon Patterson, Lisson Gallery, London
1995	*Simon Patterson,* Kohji Ogura Gallery, Nagoya
	Simon Patterson, Röntgen Kunstinstitut, Tokyo
	Midway, Artium, Fukuoka
	Sister Ships, The Customs House, South Shields
	Simon Patterson, Gandy Gallery, Prague
1994	*General Assembly,* Angel Row Gallery, Nottingham
	Simon Patterson, Kluuvin Gallery, Helsinki
	General Assembly, Chisenhale Gallery, London
1993	*Monkey Business,* The Grey Art Gallery, New York
1991	*Allahu Akbar,* Riverside Studios, London
1989	*Simon Patterson,* Third Eye Centre, Glasgow

PUBLIC COLLECTIONS

The Museum of Modern Art, New York
Tate Gallery, London
London Transport Museum, London
Victoria and Albert Museum, London
Museum of Modern Art, San Francisco
Arts Council of Great Britain, London
Wakayama Prefectural Museum MoMA, Japan
Kunsthaus, Zurich
Art Metropole, Toronto
Museum of Contemporary Art, Nagoya, Japan
The British Council Collection, London
Doncaster Museum & Art Gallery
The British Government Art Collection
Denver Art Museum
Saatchi Gallery, London

CORPORATE COLLECTIONS

Deutsche Bank Collection, London
Norton Foundation, Santa Monica
Virgin Records HQ, London
De Beers Diamonds Art Collection, London
Simmons & Simmons Collection, London
Simon BC Partners, London
BMW Art Collection, London
Riheji Corporation, Nagoya
Penguin Books Art Collection
Melitta Art Collection, Düsseldorf
Sullivan & Cromwell, Solicitors, London
British Broadcasting Corporation Collection, London
Obayashi Corporation, Tokyo

Published by Haunch of Venison
on the occasion of the exhibition
SIMON PATTERSON – BLACK-LIST
at Haunch of Venison, Zürich
28 April – 3 June 2006

HAUNCH OF VENISON

ZÜRICH
Lessingstrasse 5
8002 Zürich
Switzerland
T +41 (0)43 422 8888
F +41 (0)43 422 8889
zurich@haunchofvenison.com

LONDON
6 Haunch of Venison Yard
off Brook Street
London W1K 5ES
United Kingdom
T +44 (0)20 7495 5050
F +44 (0)20 7495 4050
london@haunchofvenison.com

www.haunchofvenison.com

Design: Juerg Judin
Photography: Jon Etter
Print: The Midas Press

Simon Patterson wishes to thank: All at Haunch of Venison,
Réka Gacs, Matt Golden, Natsue Ikeda, Alistair McClymont,
Michael Whittle and Patricia Bickers.

ISBN: 1-905620-08-X ✓